SEA·FARI DEEP

Nancy Woodman

NATIONAL
GEOGRAPHIC
SOCIETY
Washington, D.C.

Published by the National Geographic Society
1145 17th Street N.W.
Washington, D.C. 20036

John M. Fahey, Jr., President
Gilbert M. Grosvenor, Chairman of the Board
Nina D. Hoffman, Senior Vice President
William R. Gray, Vice President and
    Director of the Book Division

thanks

Library of Congress Cataloging-in-Publication Data
Woodman, Nancy.
        Sea-Fari Deep / by Nancy Woodman
p.   cm.
        Summary: In this story based on the JASON Project, Dusty joins a scientific
expedition to explore the depths of the Sea of Cortez off the coast of Baja, Mexico.
        ISBN 0-7922-7340-0
        [1. Submarines—Fiction.   2. California, Gulf of (Mexico)—Fiction.] I. Title.
PZ7.W6045Se   1999
[Fic]—dc21
97-39438

Printed in the United States of America

To~
OCEAN
GRANDMA

JASON Project

Did you know that two million school kids from around the globe join the JASON Project each year for an exciting scientific adventure? Dr. Bob Ballard, best known for his discovery of the *Titanic*, founded the JASON Project. He wanted kids to participate in his discoveries. Through state-of-the-art technology, kids at special downlink sites can communicate with scientists while watching them work and explore. They can even "fly" the remotely operated vehicle *JASON* on the ocean floor, thousands of miles away. Nancy Woodman was given special permission to join the JASON Project in the Sea of Cortez. Dusty recreates the author's real-life adventure for the reader.

The National Geographic Society is one of the founding sponsors of the JASON Project, and the Society's Grosvenor Auditorium, in Washington, D.C., is a downlink site for students.

It's hard to believe!

I went down to the bottom of the sea
and saw thermal geyser gardens, towering tube-worm forests,
and curious creatures I've never even seen pictures of....
It was the most amazing adventure I ever had!

It all started....

One day, in Uncle Wilbert's library, a book fell off the shelf and lay open saying:

"YOU ARE WHAT YOU PRETEND TO BE."

Wow, if I could be anything, what would I be? Hmmm. Maybe a whale, peacefully cruising the ocean. Or how about a famous artist like Monet or an explorer like Jacques Cousteau? Yeah! I could be an exploring adventurer, drawing pictures....

Just then Dillon, my brother, burst in with news. His class was going to study life in the sea with Dr. Bob Ballard's JASON Project. The JASON expedition would be televised live via satellite. Using computers and a state-of-the-art communication link, Dillon's class would be able to participate and ask questions of on-site scientists.

Las Animas Bay
San Francisquito Point
BAJA
San Carlos Bay
Santa Rosalia
San Ignacio Lagoon
Mulegé
Concepción Bay
CALIFORNIA
Loreto
Coronados I.
Carmen I.
Puerto Escondido
Cape San Lazaro
Magdalena Bay
Santa Margarita I.
San José I.
Amortajada Bay
Espíritu Santo I.
Pt. Lobos
La Paz
Cerralvo I.
PACIFIC OCEAN
Arena Banks
El Pulmo Reef
GORDA BANKS
Cape San Lucas

MEXICO
Guaymas
Santa Inés Bay
SEA OF CORTEZ
(GULF OF CALIFORNIA)
Agiabampo Estuary
Topolobampo
110°W
25°N

0   32   64   96   128
Scale in Miles

They'd be exploring hydrothermal vents and some weird creatures, like tube worms, that live in a deep-sea volcanic basin off the east coast of Baja California, in Mexico. The class would see pictures of the sea-floor taken by a deep-diving mini-submarine named *Turtle* and a robot, *JASON*.

Turtle - Mini Sub

A SEA-FARI! Something clicked, and I knew I had to be there. To sea... to see. Weird deep-sea creatures.... I wanted to explore their homeland and hear their stories. I wanted to watch scientists work.

Curiosity filled my mind with questions. I just had to learn more. So, I wrote to the scientists and told them I wanted to draw pictures of what they were doing and share the story with other kids.

Dr. Bob & robot JASON

TAKE ME WITH YOU!

TO: Scientists

OK!! TO: Dusty

Guess what?

Kodachrome FILM

Kodalux PROCESSING SERVICES

THEY INVITED ME ALONG!!

Meetings with Mysterious Creatures

seawater

hydrogen sulfide   minerals

minerals

hydrogen sulfide

hydrogen sulfide

seawater

DEAR ARGONAUTS,

You're invited! Join me on an amazing adventure to the very bottom of the sea to explore a newly discovered world of mysterious creatures that live without plants or light from the sun. *Fathom that!*

Plunge into the mighty Sea of Cortez with me and join SEA≈FARI DEEP!

To sea to see... Dusty

The JASON Project is named after a hero in Greek mythology. Jason was an explorer who went to sea in search of the Golden Fleece. His ship was called *Argo* and his crew the Argonauts, because they were sailors (Greek *nautes*) on the *Argo*. The mission was very difficult, but because many talented Argonauts worked together, they succeeded!

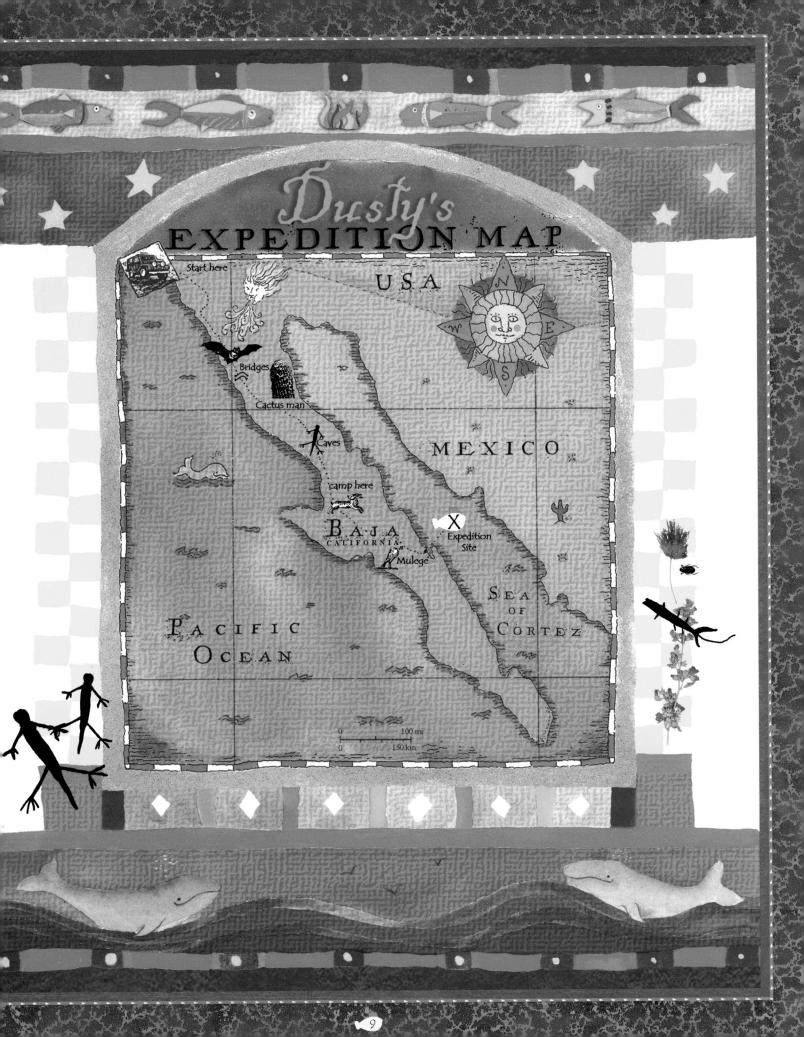

Dusty's
EXPEDITION MAP

Start here

USA

N
W E
S

Bridges

Cactus man

Caves

MEXICO

camp here

BAJA
CALIFORNIA

X
Expedition
Site

Mulege

PACIFIC
OCEAN

SEA
OF
CORTEZ

0   100 mi
0   150 km

March 1

"Baja braces itself as another major storm threatens," came a voice from the early morning news.

It was still dark when I was waking up in Coronado, California.

"Time to hit the road!" Uncle Wilbert called. "We've got to beat the storm and cross the bridges before the rains hit or you'll miss the expedition!"

I bounded out of bed, dressed, and threw my gear in the Jeep. Great adventurers never travel anywhere without a good-luck charm, so I grabbed Max, my lucky "ugligator," and stuffed him into my pocket. We waved good-bye to Dillon and headed south.

The sun was just coming up as we crossed into Mexico.

cave painting

Hola Dillon!
Here we are in Mexico.
Made it across the
bridges just in time before
the storm. Yikes–close call! It's
really different here –strange-
looking cactus everywhere! The
rain has turned the desert into
a paintbox of color! We camped
hear a cave. It's beautiful...
and spooky at night! I'm
glad Uncle Wilbert decided
to drive me to Baja. He's
excited about going whale
watching when I go out to
sea.
Yipeee!!! Wish you
were here!
Your awesome sister,
Dusty
p.s. The iguanas love Max...

Max & the Ocotillo

March 4
Sea of Cortez

I'm here! I saluted toward a small boat at the
end of a lonely pier in Mulegé and ran past the
vulture patrol perched on a lone cactus. It was time
to "transit" out to DSVSS *Laney Chouest,* a ship used
by the U.S. Navy at the expedition site.

"We might be in for a rough ride," the captain
reported. "Make sure your life jackets are secure."

I waved good-bye to Uncle Wilbert as we pulled away from
the pier. Our 26-foot boat felt awfully small on the open sea.

A pod of dolphins hurried across our path, bounding
over the waves. A gray whale spouted in the
distance. The bold mountain landscape
disappeared. Sometimes you have to lose sight
of one shore to find another, I remember my
uncle saying.

BYE-BYE

gray whale

Our sea world was like a giant
roller-coaster of MAJOR WAVES
that grew more humongous
by the minute.

"Here comes a big one," yelled the
captain. "Hold on!" Whoahhhhh....
The boat rolled, and we landed in a heap.
Waves washed over the rail.

"Ooowww...that water is COLD!" gargled a photographer
with a mouthwash of waves.

"The Sea of Cortez is unpredictable," the captain yelled.
"She can be as gentle as a minnow one minute and
as fierce as a hungry barracuda the next! We're headed
toward that orange speck on the horizon."

After two and a half hours of being tossed by wet walls
of water, we finally reached the *Laney Chouest*, 22 miles
offshore. A small inflatable raft, a Zodiac, was
sent to greet us.

One by one we jumped from the side of our
rocking boat into the bouncing lap of the Zodiac,
six feet below. A Zodiac diver caught me so I wouldn't
go tumbling into the raging sea. "Hold on!" he said.

Then we were off like a bucking bronco.

When we pulled alongside the *Laney Chouest*, I jumped
from the Zodiac to the ship's iron ladder and scrambled away
from the jaws of the hungry sea.

"It was nice of you to shower before coming to see us," the
crew laughed as they helped us out of our dripping life vests.

"Hey Dusty," came a voice from around the maze
of equipment. It was Eddie, my expedition
sponsor. I recognized him from a photo.

"Come with me to the control room.
We're getting some great pictures
from *JASON*."

The Control Room

As my eyes adjusted to the dark room,
Eddie introduced me to the team of scientists
working on the project.

"This is Martin—he's the pilot 'flying' our remotely operated
vehicle (ROV), JASON. Next to Martin is Rich. He's
studying 'bugs,' the creatures living in the hydrothermal
vent community. Véronique is creating a geologic map
of the area through computer imaging."

On the monitor, through JASON's camera eye, we
could see down 7,000 feet to the seafloor.

"Wow!" I gasped, "Awesome!" There were thousands
of tube worms; massive forests of white tubular
bodies with feathery, red, lipstick-tube heads.

The camera drifted along sloped walls of tube-
worm forests—a wondrous, peaceful dreamland,
untouched and unspoiled. I was surprised how
white the tube worms were; how fresh and
unbattered by the sea they looked.

WHO'S WHO

Laney
Chouest   A

Turtle   B

Medea   C

JASON   D

TO VENTS

From the control room of the
Laney Chouest (A) scientists
are able to watch pictures
from ROV JASON (D), a
robot, as well as monitor
the positions of its
camera sled, Medea (C),
and Turtle (B), a three-
person mini-sub.

16

EARTH EVENTS
4.6 Billion Years Ago-Earth formed.
1.2 Billion Years Ago-earliest
known animal fossils deposited
(jellyfish-like creatures).
180 Million Years Ago-the
Continent Pangaea began to
break because of shifting
plates.
65 Million Years Ago-
dinosaurs became extinct.
14 Million Years Ago-Sea of Cortez
formed as Baja California
separated from
the mainland.

PANGAEA

"You're looking at the Guaymas Basin," said Eddie, "an amazing hydrothermal vent site."

"What is a hydrothermal vent, anyhow? How is it formed?" I asked.

"The surface of the Earth is made up of plates that move around because of changes deep inside," Véronique answered. "The San Andreas Fault runs through California into the Sea of Cortez. But it is not a single, straight fault. It is segmented. In between the segments the plates are slowly spreading apart about two inches a year. Hot magma from deep in the Earth comes up through fissures, or cracks. It hits the cold seawater, and wham, it hardens and cracks. Then cold seawater seeps way down deep into the fissures where it is very hot. Because of the intense heat, minerals are leached from the hardened rock and dissolve into the seawater. Like a geyser erupting, the mineral-rich, scalding water is forced back up and gushes through the seafloor in openings called vents. 'Hydrothermal' is another way of saying 'hot water.'"

· Earth's Tectonic Plates ·

The Surface of the earth is made up of plates that
move, causing continents to shift. They move at
about the rate your fingernails grow.

minerals

hydrogen sulfide

seawater

seawater

minerals

minerals

hydrogen sulfide

hydrogen sulfide

Tube-worm Forest

"We are seeing some pretty weird creatures living down there without energy from the sun," said Rich. "Until these vents were discovered, no one had ever seen anything like them. The creatures live off of bacteria that use chemical energy to make sugar. That's called chemosynthesis. Until very recently we thought that animals needed plants to survive, but in hydrothermal vent communities there are NO PLANTS!

"Here's how chemosynthesis works. When vent water that has been heated by geothermal energy and enriched with hydrogen sulfide comes in contact with seawater, the hydrogen sulfide in it is broken down, or oxidized, and energy is released. For animals to use this energy, it must first be captured by bacteria. This is chemosynthesis in action. It is similar to photosynthesis, the process plants use when they take energy from the sun to produce sugar for food. In chemosynthesis the bacteria use geothermal energy rather than solar energy to produce sugar."

"It sounds like an ecosystem that's really different from the one we live in," I thought out loud.

"Those animals can live whether the sun is shining or not! Wow, maybe there is something we can learn from them...."

Hydrogen sulfide is released from a vent (yellow arrow) and is used by the bacteria inside the tube worm (green arrow) to produce sugar.

"We've already learned a lot," said Rich. "We're using some of the bacteria and thermophilic microbes—heat-loving microscopic life-forms— found in the vents for eating up oil slicks, for medical research, and in genetic engineering. We're also trying to use them to come up with new sources of energy.

"Who knows, maybe the vents will help us find another way to run our cars! Microbes are probably the oldest life-forms on Earth. It's possible that they exist on other planets!"

PHOTOSYNTHESIS

Solar Energy

Plant Leaf

Plants use sunlight to make sugar. In the process they give off oxygen.

CHEMOSYNTHESIS

Bacteria

Geothermal Energy

Bacteria use geothermal energy to make sugar. In the process they give off Sulfate.

Theory: There may be a biosphere of microbes, or "river of slime," that circulates miles beneath the earth's surface. A few million microbes could fit on the head of a pin!

Nummie!

Muck

OIL

Nasty Pollutants

Microbe

Microbes eat yucky stuff and clean the environment.

Circulating Biosphere Theory

Volcano

mantle

geysers

inner core

outer core

circulating microbes

Smokers

mines

"Look, what's THAT?" Véronique shouted.

Soon, every eye was glued to the monitor. A strange looking creature loped across the ocean floor. It was actually translucent. We were seeing its insides!

To propel its body forward, it used its legs to push off, jack-rabbit fashion. This little guy was probably a new species of deep-sea octopus making his television debut in front of thousands of people, including Dillon's class! His unexpected performance had us clapping wildly.

As the camera focused on the side of a huge, chimney-like formation called a black smoker, Rich said, "This little character, named *Alvinella pompijana*, is one of my favorites!"

black coral

And I could see why. It was one of the weirdest creatures I have ever seen.

alvinella
Pompeii worm
lives on smokers

Alvinella pompijana

a species of Graneledone octopus

JASON's temperature probe read 122°F (50°C) at *Alvinella's* "house," and went up to 572°F (300°C) as it was inserted into the mouth of the black smoker. Blackish, mineral-rich water encircled the probe.

"Véronique, we learned in school that water turns into a gas when it boils at 212°F (100°C). Why is the 572°F water coming out of the smoker still liquid?" I asked.

At 662°F (350°C) vent fluid is hot enough to glow.

"The boiling point of water is much higher on the seafloor because of the extreme pressure there," Véronique said. "When vent water hits the surrounding 34°F (1°C) water, it cools quickly. As it cools, minerals, such as iron, zinc, and copper sulfides, precipitate—or 'rain down'—and attach to the smokers. This causes them to grow taller. We have seen them as tall as a 15-story building!"

They look a little like the sand castles you build by dribbling wet sand through your fingers....

WOW

"Godzilla" → tallest smoker found at another site in the North Pacific Ocean.

Laney
Chouest

Martin explained how *JASON* brings pictures to us.

"*JASON* can be 'flown' from the control room by a pilot or a computer. A fiber optic cable connects *JASON* to the *Laney Chouest*. The cable is only as wide as a finger and contains three glass fibers. One of the fibers is used to control *JASON*'s movements from the control room. Pulses of laser light are sent through the other two fibers to carry information and images from *JASON* to the control room. From there, the images go to the production room."

"Let's head over there and see what happens next," Eddie said.

JASON

Pilot "flying" JASON

Vents
1½ miles↓

Student "flying" JASON from a down-link site

Downlink site at the National Geographic Society

The Production Room

"4...3...2...1..., you're on," the cameraman said. Dr. Bob Ballard greeted thousands of kids at downlink sites thousands of miles away through the eye of the camera. As leader of the expedition, Dr. Bob was explaining telepresence and how it works.

"The ship's lab was wired as a TV production facility. Here a television crew selects images coming from *JASON*. The pictures are sent in the form of a microwave signal to a satellite, Galaxy 7, orbiting 22,500 miles above the Equator.

"In less than a second students at downlink sites are able to see what is actually happening. They can talk to shipboard scientists and 'fly' *JASON* using a specially installed joystick! This sense of being there we call telepresence. Scientists join us here while sitting in their laboratories at home!"

This is how Dillon's class watches and participates, I thought as Eddie and I tiptoed from the room.

Galaxy 7

To Downlink Sites

A Downlink Site

Laney Chouest

Medea

JASON

1. JASON collects images from the seafloor.
2. Images travel through a cable to the ship's
3. control room where scientists operate JASON and monitor images going to the
4. production room. A television crew selects images and sends them to a satellite,
5. Galaxy 7, which sends them to a
6. broadcasting company and then on to an
7. information management center where they are uplinked to the
8. satellite and beamed down to
9. downlink sites ... all in less than a second!

March 5
Turtle

We found *Turtle* in a hanger near the stern of the *Laney Chouest*. The pilot was inside checking the systems....

Ho Dillon!
I'm here! This is my new friend Turtle! She's a 26-ft. mini-sub that can dive almost 2 miles deep. Inside there's a thick steel sphere with room for a 3-person crew. It is strong enough to with-stand 49,215 tons of pressure. Can you imagine 8,200 elephants standing on your head? Turtle has manipulator arms with pinchers on the end to collect samples from the seafloor and place them in a collection box. And, guess what else - there's something like your monster squirt gun called a slurp gun - it slurps up small creatures and sediment from the bottom to study later on. Also, Turtle has a video camera for underwater filming. And, oh, remember Capt. Nemo's window in Twenty Thousand Leagues Under the Sea? Well, Turtle has 3 of those viewports to the deep. They're only 5" in diameter, but 4½" thick! Each one can withstand a half million pounds of pressure. That's a lot!

C U later, alligator, Dusty

P.S. Max has a new buddy, too...

Max + Shamu

← Turtle's mascot

camera lens

About Turtle...
The Navy people affection-ately call Turtle "toy" because she is so small compared to other sub-marines.
Turtle runs on batteries and is equipped with a CO_2 scrubber, a system that removes carbon dioxide from the air, since it is toxic for humans to breathe in concentration. Life support in the mini-sub could last for about three days.

hatch
long baseline acoustic transducer
radio antenna
propeller
Turtle back (flotation)
Sail
fathometer
TURTLE
Side lift Pod
lights
shamu
camera
light
viewport
side viewport
manipulator arm

More about Turtle...
If Turtle were to lose power on a dive, she can release the weights that helped her sink to the bottom. Turtle's batteries can also be blown off. Then, if necessary, a guillotine can cut off the heavy manipulator arms. After dropping all that weight, she would be light enough to surface.

Manipulator arm's pincher

Slurp gun

PB4UGO

Manipulator arm pouring water

Rick, the pilot, came out of *Turtle* and saluted Eddie. "We've finished our pre-dive check. We're all powered up and systems are go. Only one problem: We're short a passenger."

Eddie winked at me. "Hey, Dusty, would you like to go?"

"REALLY?" I danced, feeling so excited I almost burst.

"Before you go, though, let's draw some pictures on these Styrofoam cups. We'll attach them to the outside of *Turtle* to see if the dive changes them."

4½"

The Dive

Waves of excitement tickled me. What would it be like to go down in a submersible?

On deck a U.S. Navy commander gave a pre-dive briefing. "*Turtle* will be piloted by Lt. Rick, and the observers will be scientist Rose and special scientist-in-training Dusty. Your job, Dusty, is to draw pictures of what you see and to create a story that can be shared with all the kids who would like to be in your place!

"*Turtle* will be diving to a depth of 1,135 fathoms (6,810 feet), at 27° 0' 55" north latitude, 111° 24' 55" west longitude," he announced.

Wow, I guess we're really going to do it, I thought to myself and squeezed Max. Sketch pad, pen, PB&J sandwich, sweatshirt...well, I guess that's all I need.

Expedition Map

Mexico

Sea of Cortez

— 100 miles —

Northern Trench

Guaymas

385

Guaymas

905   1010
       1110
170   855   1015   905   830   653   385   167   10
                                              315   40
      800   1135   848   636
190   653   737   995   1010
10   413   Southern
40   Basin   Trench
          620   1040   670
                   1005   580
          980

890   Depths in fathoms

N

Mulege

Baja
CALIFORNIA

We filed up the ladder, hydronauts ready to explore the unknown.

At 1:15 p.m. (1315 they say aboard the ship) we took off our shoes and climbed down the hatch.

"Even a human hair in the seal of the hatch could cause a leak," Rick told us as he examined it carefully. Good-bye fresh air, I thought as he battened down the hatch. We were sealed in!

Inside the mini-sub there were zillions of buttons, switches, lights, and not much room for us! It was like being inside a ball that is about six feet across.

Rose and I sat on a bench. "What if I have to go to the bathroom?" I whispered.

"That's what these Piddle-Paks are for," she said, holding up a plastic bag....

← hatch

steel sphere in Turtle

Zodiac divers

Human Hair

HATCH

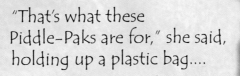

Piddle-Pak

sponge

TURTLE

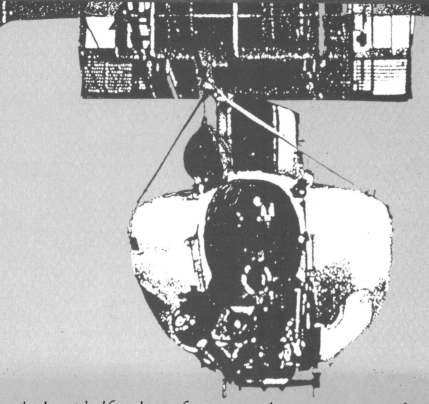

It took about half an hour for *Laney Chouest's* giant A-frame hoist to grab onto the 24-ton *Turtle*, swing us over the stern, and slowly lower us into the water. I was glued to the viewport, watching blue sky turn into turquoise as we plunged into the sea. Suddenly, we were bobbing in the waves, and two divers from the Zodiac were disconnecting us from the hoist. Rick was busy checking gauges to make sure seawater was not leaking in. "Ready, sir," Rick radioed to the control center.

"*Turtle*, you're cleared to dive."

"Have fun," a diver radioed from above. "We're out of here." There was a big splash out the viewport as the divers swam away. We were on our own.

Rick flipped a power switch and flooded the ballast tanks. *Turtle* started to sink. Good-bye world above the sea.... WE'RE GOING DOWN!

I took a deep breath, scared and excited at the same time. It was like being in an underwater elevator with no doors. The turquoise sea turned cobalt blue as we descended toward darkness. Wide-eyed fish swam by, as if wondering what kind of sea monster we might be.

At 300 feet the motor quit. We were sinking! The depth gauge was dropping quickly. Uh-oh. I gulped hard and tried to act cool. "What's going on?" I whispered, trying not to let the weight of my words take us deeper.

I looked out the viewport, but darkness was surrounding us and all I could see was my worried reflection. I squeezed Max hard.

"Oh, it's OK, Dusty." Rick explained, "We're pumping oil into the ballast to replace some of the seawater. Since oil is lighter than water, *Turtle* won't be so heavy. When we reach what's called neutral buoyancy, the sub will stop sinking, and we'll just sort of float. Then we'll use our side motors to help us go up and down."

"Oh," I answered, acting calm but thinking, PHEW! that's a relief.

manta ray

ZONES of the OCEAN

sea level
Epipelagic
200 meters
Mesopelagic
1000 meters
Bathypelagic
Abyssopelagic
4,000 meters

1 meter = 3.28 feet

ctenophore

comb jelly

They're on the glow!

When the depth gauge read 1,100 feet, it was pitch-black outside, and something strange happened. I saw twinkles in the darkness.

"That's bioluminescence," Rose said. "We're now in the bathypelagic zone of the ocean. 'Bathy' means 'deep' in Greek. Tiny creatures out there produce their own light, like fireflies of the deep."

It was a magical kingdom, all right. Fantastic shapes—twisting and turning in a glorious underwater ballet; glittering and shimmering in a jet-black sea.

"What makes them glow?" I asked Rose.

"Their light is the result of a chemical reaction from substances they secrete. We call bioluminescence cold light because, unlike fire, the light gives off no heat. It helps the creatures attract food or mates, defend themselves, and see."

Atolla

Bargmannia

In the deep ocean red appears black. Many jellies are red, making them invisible to their predators.

"Oh, look at that squiggly worm," Rick said.

Looking more closely, though, it was
the intestine of a transparent creature radiating
an eerie blue light.

"Wow, what's that?" I asked Rose, as another
creature caught my eye.

"That's a comb jelly, a type of jellyfish. It swims
by vibrating hairlike combs, or cilia. The cilia
appear to glow. They reflect light at different angles,
creating a rainbow of sparkling colors," she replied.
We'll catch one with the slurp gun on the way up
and take it back to study."

I lost sight of the glowing creatures. All I could
see was total darkness as we continued down.
There was nothing, nothing but the sound of bubbles
and the whir of motors. *Turtle's* soft,
amber light barely lit our sphere.
It looked like the cockpit of
a plane flying at night.

Pelagic worm

Agmayeria

comb jelly

Periphylla

In some languages "jellyfish"
means "living water."

Benthocodon

Suddenly, a cold chill went down my back, and then another. It felt wet, like water. WATER??!! I looked up, and a drip splashed in my face.

There was water dripping off the hatch!

Then I noticed water collecting on the viewport!! OH, NO...were we leaking? WERE WE DOOMED? Terror sirens went off in my body. "Rick! Rick!..." I cried, trying not to sound too hysterical. My eyes darted around the sphere, desperately searching for a crack. It was cool, but I started to sweat.

Rick was busy logging information and cocked his head toward me without looking over. "Uh-huh."

"Rick, water is dripping down my back. I think we might have a leak..." I gasped.

Seconds seemed like forever. My heart moved up into my throat, and the beats echoed through my body, throbbing through every cell. *Thud, thud, thud.* Even my swallow stood still, waiting... waiting....

Finally Rick responded.

"Uh-huh. Well, taste the water. If it's salty, then we have a problem. If it's not, then it's just condensation forming on the hatch."

Then Rick started to send a message to the ship in Morse code.

What was he saying? Was it an SOS?

I tilted my head back and waited for a drop to fall into my mouth, thinking that my life depended on its taste. I closed my eyes, tuned up my taste buds, and waited for the end.

Finally, the drop came. I sloshed it around in my mouth and prayed. Hmmm, no salty taste. Another drop, and then another. It was pure, fresh water!

Aaahhhhh. My heart floated back into my chest.

We descended in darkness for two hours to the seafloor.

Then Rick turned on the outside lights and there, in front of our eyes, was a dazzling world of tube worms, underwater chimneys, and huge rock formations. I could barely speak. Here we were, more than a mile below the surface of the sea; three privileged aliens, close-up visitors to this incredible world of weird and fantastic creatures.

A gentle current flowed through the underwater fairyland; it was like watching music.

I held Max up to the viewport.
"Can you believe this?"

Rick maneuvered *Turtle*, being careful to stay clear of the hydrothermal vent fluid. At 662°F (350°C) the fluid was hot enough to melt *Turtle*'s viewports.

"What's that?" I asked Rose. The video monitor was giving us an image of a huge rock mushroom.

"That's a 'pagoda.' It's a black smoker with a 'roof.' Hydrothermal vent fluid flowing out from under the roof is trapped as it tries to rise. It looks like an upside-down waterfall, doesn't it?

"There is a temperature difference of 608°F (320°C) between the top of the pagoda's roof and the underneath side—and they're only 5 inches apart!

"That sparkly white stuff on the pagoda is anhydrite, or calcium sulfide. We can watch this mineral being formed right before our eyes! It's created when vent water, which contains sulfate, mixes with calcium in the seawater."

The pagoda shimmered in the dark.

Could Monet have ever imagined such a beautiful water garden without plants?

We turned into a tube-worm forest. WOW, stunning!

"Tube worms are animals that live only near hydrothermal vents," Rose told me. "They're the star players in this chemosynthetic ecosystem. Like other animals, they're born with a mouth. But very early in life, they lose their mouth and gut as certain bacteria grow in their systems. These bacteria have a special relationship with tube worms called a symbiotic relationship. This means the bacteria and the tube worms both benefit in some way from living together.

"The bacteria absorb (metabolize) hydrogen sulfide, which is highly toxic to most other animals.

"In doing so they create sugar and provide the tube worm with energy. The bacteria benefits by being given a safe environment inside the tube worm to grow and collect nutrients. Tube worms grow to be eight feet tall in some vent communities."

3'-8'!

25 new families of creatures have been found in vent communities: 100 new species. The nearest relative to some of these species lived more than 250 million years ago in the Paleozoic era.

TUBEWORM

Oxygen
Hydrogen
sulfide
Carbon
dioxide

Tentacle

Muscle

Trophosome
with
bacteria

Blood
vessels

Tube worm
tube

Giant lithodid crabs "tiptoed" among the tube worms. Thermal geyser gardens of black smokers towered over us, some 40 feet tall. I grabbed my sketch pad and started to draw.

Rose pointed out a huge colony of clams. "In some vent communities, the clams are as big as a foot long! They grow quickly, almost two inches a year. That's probably because vent communities don't last long. Eruptions and earthquakes along spreading zones can wipe them out. Clams need to colonize rapidly to insure their survival."

A tube worm is both male & female. Eggs and sperm are released into the seawater. Larvae form and float in the ocean current to their new home.

Lithodid crab has a 12" leg span

Mmm steamed clams!

Clams as big as dinnerplates!

We floated over a field of bright yellow "mat" bacteria called Beggiatoa. "They're different from the bacteria that live inside the tube worms and clams. Crabs and other creatures graze on mat bacteria, which form the basis of the food chain," Rose told me.

Rick deftly used *Turtle*'s manipulator arm to collect samples for Rose to study later.

We started down a canyon wall through jagged rock formations. Rick watched the monitor while Rose looked out the viewport.

Mat bacteria

1.

2.

3.

Types of bacteria
1. Plume bacteria live in the cloudy water that flows from the vents.
2. Symbiotic bacteria live in tube worms and clams.
3. Mat bacteria, Beggiatoa, form slimy mats on surfaces around the vents.

"Be careful, there's a big...." THUD! Before Rose could finish, *Turtle* jolted and shook. Rocks showered around us. We had run into a pagoda, and it broke into pieces, bombarding us with debris.

We all looked at each other with our mouths wide open and then looked around the sphere to see if everything was intact. I couldn't get it out of my mind that a pinhole stream of water would have enough pressure to go right through bone.

Breaking the tension, Rick said, "I bet *Turtle* will need a Band-Aid when we get back."

Inside a Smoker

Véronique's geologic map. We are here.

pagoda

← Magma

After awhile we had lunch—there's nothing like peanut butter and jelly at 6,700 feet below the surface of the sea.

Then Rick collected more samples, Rose wrote her observations, and I had a chance to draw more weird creatures.

Time flew by. Our bottom time was up. We dropped ballast and started our two-hour journey home. I closed my eyes and visions of tube worms danced in my head.

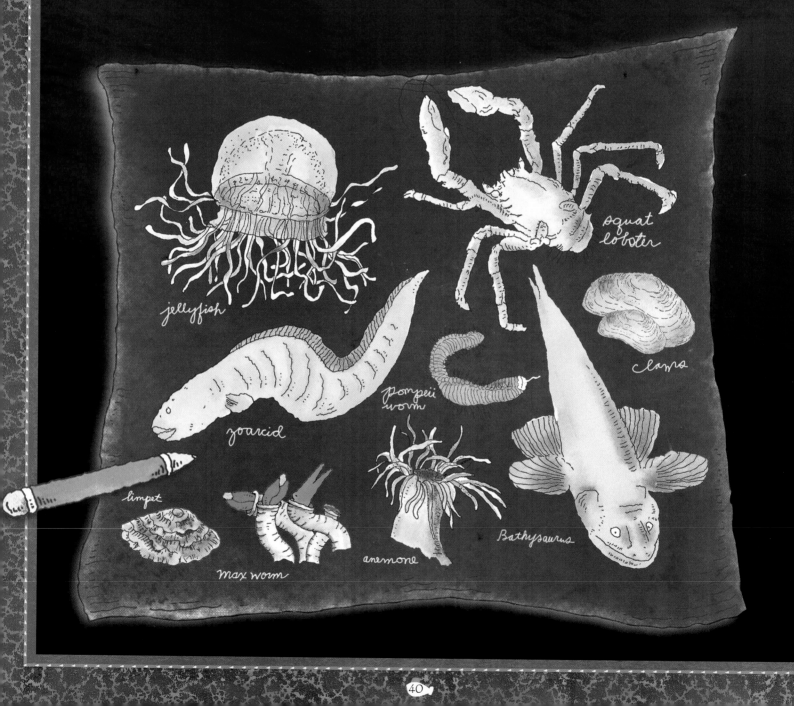

jellyfish

squat lobster

claws

zoarcid

pompeii worm

limpet

max worm

anemone

Bathysaurus

We rose slowly through the darkness, a hundred feet per minute, and surfaced just in time to see the setting sun.

Rick flipped on *Turtle*'s external lights, and we emerged like a glowing bubble. We bobbled like a tiny bobber on an endless blue sea. The Zodiac divers appeared, ready to haul us in. *Turtle* was captured, soon to be hoisted aboard the *Laney Chouest*. As she approached, it appeared she might swallow us. Then we felt a sudden jolt, and *WHOOSH,* we were snagged by the grippers on the ship's hoist. *Turtle* was flying!

We were HOME.

We had just experienced a wilderness that few have ever encountered.

I knew at that moment that my life had changed forever. I looked at the drawings on my lap and hoped that they'd show other kids even half of what I felt. Like an astronaut who views the Earth from afar or walks on the moon, I would never again be able to view the world in the same way.

Ahoy Dillon! Argonaut-Hydronaut
Dusty, checking in ~ just surfaced from
Sea~Fari Deep! A surprise was waiting
for me as I climbed down from Turtle's
ladder. SWOOOSH! The crew sent
buckets of seawater flying to greet me as my
initiation to the Turtle Dive Club. It's a tradition - I'm an
official hydronaut now! The dive was incredible ... I can
understand why Uncle Wilbert is a marine biologist. The sea
is full of wondrous things - it's so mysterious and enchanting ...
can't wait to tell you about my adventure!

Over and out, Dusty

P.S. You won't believe what happened to the Styrofoam cups attached to
Turtle...

HYDRONAUT

This is to certify that

Dusty

designated Honorary Hydronaut.
corded all honors, rights and
befit those daring souls that
venture into the depths of the realm of
Neptunus Rex. Be it known that this exalted
status was earned on 9 March by
descending 3009' feet into Davy Jones's
locker in the U.S. Navy Deep Submergence
Vessel TURTLE.

NEPTUNUS REX
RULER OF THE RAGING MAIN
BY HIS SERVANT

ATTEST FOR DAVY JONES

PILOT

OIC DSV TURTLE

Turtle's owie

SEA OF CORTEZ
JASON PROJECT
VOYAGE IV
TEAM TURTLE

DSV-3 TURTLE
EX-729-30-6

1"

JASON 27° 0.55 N
111° 24.55'

DUSTY
9 March

Back ashore I sat down on the sand,
feeling warm all over. Next to my
sketch pad and paints was my journal
just waiting to hear my story.
I picked up a pen
and began...

Glossary

Argonaut   a sailor on the *Argo*, a ship that according to Greek mythology was used by Jason to explore the seas in search of the hide of a golden ram; any participant in a JASON Project expedition

bacteria   a group of one-celled microscopic organisms; chief food-producers in a hydrothermal vent community

ballast   a heavy material that is placed in the hold of a ship to improve stability

bioluminescence   light produced by living organisms

chemosynthesis   the process by which bacteria combine water and carbon dioxide with energy from hydrogen sulfide or other chemicals to make food

condensation   the change of a substance, such as water, from a gas to a liquid

downlink site   a place where students can participate through telepresence with the JASON Project

ecosystem   a term used in classifying the Earth's natural communities according to how organisms and their environments function as a unit

fault   a break in the Earth's crust along which movement up, down, or sideways occurs

fiber optic cable   a bundle of hair-thin transparent rods of glass or plastic through which light energy is transmitted; used in the transmission of images from *JASON* to the *Laney Chouest*

fissure   an open crack in the Earth's crust

geothermal energy   energy that comes from within the Earth

geyser   a spring through which hot water and steam erupt

hydrogen sulfide   a gas that is used by bacteria to produce food for organisms living in a hydrothermal vent community

hydronaut   a term for a person who travels underwater to explore

hydrothermal vents   openings in the seafloor through which mineral-rich hot water comes out

latitude   the distance north or south of the Equator; represented on a globe or map by lines that run parallel to the Equator

leaching   the process by which water picks up mineral elements or compounds as it passes through another substance

longitude   the distance east or west of the prime meridian; represented on a globe or map by lines that run north and south

magma   a very hot liquid within the Earth that, when cooled, forms rocks

metabolize   the means by which chemical reactions within an organism create energy from food

microwave	a comparatively short, high-frequency radio wave
neutral buoyancy	point at which a submersible will float underwater, neither sinking nor rising
pagoda	a kind of black smoker that has a roof shaped like a Chinese temple
Pangaea	in the theory of plate tectonics, a single supercontinent that scientists believe began to split apart approximately 200 million years ago to eventually form the present continents
photosynthesis	process by which green plants use energy from sunlight to combine water and carbon dioxide to make food and oxygen
plates	in geology, thick, slow-moving slabs of crust that form our planet and hold the continents and the ocean basins
precipitate	to cause to separate from solution
ROV	a term that means "remotely operated vehicle;" a robot, like *JASON*
smoker	an active hydrothermal vent where plumes of mineral-rich hot water gush from the vent opening, eventually creating a chimney around the vent; in a black smoker the plume is black
submersible	a small underwater craft, like *Turtle*, that is used especially for deep-sea research
symbiotic relationship	two organisms living together in a manner that benefits both
telepresence	the sense of "being there" conveyed by real-time video transmission of images and sounds
thermophilic microbes	heat-loving microscopic organisms

Image Credits

Unless otherwise noted the following credits refer to photographs:

pp. 6 right (art), 38 left (bacteria art), reprinted with permission from *Baja California Sur JASON Curriculum*. Copyright © 1992 by the National Science Teachers Association; pp. 7 far left (art), 10 left (logo), courtesy JASON Project; pp. 7 lower left, 7 lower center, 30 (all photos), 31 up left, lower left, lower right, 30 (all photos), 31 up left, lower left, lower right, Laurence P. Madin, Woods Hole Oceanographic Institute; pp. 7 lower right (diagram), 17 lower right (diagram), 18 lower left (art), courtesy *American Scientist*; pp. 7 center right (both), 11 left, 14 left (both), 15 up right, 16 up right, 25 lower right, 26 up left, 47 left, Robert Dashiell; p. 10 Jeep art based on

photograph by Martin Litton; p.11 up left, courtesy Don Baker *Outside Magazine*; pp. 16 left (art), 17 up right and up center (diagrams), 19 up (art), 22 up center (art), 23 right (art), 40 all (art), based on material in *Baja California Sur JASON Curriculum*. Copyright © 1992 by the National Science Teachers Association; p. 18 up left, Richard A. Lutz, Rutgers University, Institute of Marine and Coastal Sciences; pp. 20 lower right, 20–21 lower, 21 lower center, 41, Emory Kristof NGP; pp. 21 left, 21 up right, 36 lower left, Al Giddings; 21 lower right (art), based on material in article by V. Robigou, et al., in *Geophysical Research Letters*, Vol. 20, 1993; p. 22 lower center, Mark O. Thiessen NGP, lower right, Todd A. Gipstein NGP; pp. 25 right center (both), 27 lower right, 29 up right, courtesy U.S. Navy; p. 28 lower left, Eddie Luchs, U.S. Navy; 29 lower right, Amos Nachoum; p. 36 lower right, Peter Lonsdale, Scripps Institution of Oceanography; p. 38 up left, Frederick Grassle, Rutgers University, Institute of Marine and Coastal Sciences; p. 39 up right, Rodney Catanach, Woods Hole Oceanographic Institute; 39 lower (map art), based on material in article by V. Robigou and R. D. Ballard in *EOS* magazine, Vol. 75, 1994; p. 47 right Ron Roehmholdt; all other photographs and artwork by Nancy Woodman (e-mail address: FoxbrierNW@aol.com)

Yikes! There are at least 226 *Turtles* on each page!

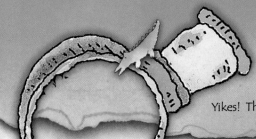

Thanks, fellow ARGONAUTS

Robert Dashiell, digital teammate/photographer

Scientists: Véronique Robigou, University of Washington, School of Oceanography; Fred Grassle, Richard Lutz, Rose Petrecca, and Waldo Wakefield, Rutgers University, Institute of Coastal and Marine Sciences; Martin Bowen, Holger Jannasch, Laurence Madin, Carl Wirsen, and Dana Yoerger, Woods Hole Oceanographic Institute; Cindy Lee Van Dover, College of William and Mary; Janet Voight, Chicago Field Museum; Bruce Robison, Monterey Bay Research Institute; Peter Lonsdale and Richard Rosenblatt, Scripps Institution of Oceanography

Turtle crew members, especially Eddie Luchs; The National Science Teachers Association; *American Scientist* magazine; Ron Roehmholdt, Keyport Undersea Museum; Jennifer Emmett, Suzanne Fonda, Charles Kogod, Marianne Koszorus, Lyle Rosbotham, Vince Ryan, and Jim Sorensen, National Geographic Society

Dr. Robert Ballard, Cathy Offinger, and Tim Armour, JASON Foundation for Education; and The JASON Project (Web site:www.jasonproject.org)

Appreciation to Margaret Sampson, David Gaddis, Violette Fitzgerald, Millye Mills, Bonnie Vicks, Joe Ochlak, Quad Graphics, and David Seager

About Max...

A free-spirited, world-traveling companion to the author, Max holds the world record for the deepest dive by an "ugligator." With an insatiable appetite for adventure, Max's curiosity often finds him in places where ugligators are not commonly known to visit. A keen environmentalist, Max spends much of his at-home time promoting environmental and endangered species issues, subjects he believes in dearly since he is the last (albeit only) ugligator known to exist.

About the author...

I began journaling when I was 11, recording thoughts, feelings, drawings, and observations about nature. A goal is to make a new discovery each day. My expeditions take me to far-away places or to one square foot of earth at home, on the Olympic Peninsula. I've discovered the world can be found in a grain of sand. There's always an adventure within reach.

About the book...

Without Squidzilla, my computer, this book would not have been possible. Sea-Fari Deep is one of the first children's books to be submitted to National Geographic in digital form. I created the paintings, then scanned and assembled them digitally. This allowed me to combine pastels, watercolors, and photographic images into one piece of art. Wow, dealing with Squid's personality is a whole story in itself!

nanneroo